Toward A New Afrikan Revolution: Volume I

Reflections on the Struggle for Black Freedom and Self-Determination

Khalid Raheem

ABSTRACT:

This book represents a collection of my thoughts and ideas, new and previously shared, regarding some of the challenges facing the current effort and work to obtain freedom and liberation for Black people within the United States. It is not meant nor intended to be an academic study, but rather a series of observations, experiences and interpretations. I encourage readers to engage in debate, serious research and discourse concerning the many comments presented. I look forward to constructive criticism and feedback. The first chapter deals with definitions and how they can either help us in getting things done or keep us spinning in endless circles. Chapter 2 shares perspective about independent politics. In Chapter 3, I present critical commentary concerning the Black Lives Matter network and movement. In Chapter 4, I discuss some of the limitations imposed by certain ideologies which have been popular among Black activists. Chapter 5 is a reflection on the Black Panther Party. Chapter 6 takes on the role of Black military and police. Chapter 7 provides suggestions for further developing and strengthening the movement. And, finally Chapter 8 presents a series of select writings between the years 2014 and 2017.

Toward A New Afrikan Revolution: Volume I

Reflections on the Struggle for

Black Freedom

And

Self-Determination

BY

KHALID RAHEEM

FOREWORD:

A few years ago, as part of the ongoing political education initiative of the New Afrikan Independence Party (NAIP), I developed a pamphlet titled 'The Philosophy and Platform of the New Afrikan Independence Party'. This pamphlet continues to serve as an introduction to and basic explanation of the Party's focus and platform.

This is actually my first foray into writing any sort of book, in this instance, a collection of my thoughts regarding various aspects of the ongoing struggle for Black liberation and freedom.

Our communities face a host of serious challenges today that are indeed very similar to those faced by the generations of the middle-to-late twentieth century: white-supremacy, racism, mass-incarceration, police violence and misconduct, wealth-disparity, sexism and income inequality.

We are also living during a period of serious conflict and contradiction among elements of the ruling-class elite of the United States and even among some of their main allies abroad. Capitalism is in crisis. Neo-liberalism is proving to be unable and unwilling to fulfill its promise. White nationalism and authoritarianism have gained political ground throughout the United States, Europe and certain parts of Latin America.

This edition of 'Toward A New Afrikan Revolution' is an attempt to offer some perspective and perhaps some sense of direction for all of those who are impacted by the reality of being Black in America and those of us who identify ourselves as activist, radicals, revolutionaries and people of conscience.

I want to thank the Supporters, Brothers, Sisters and Comrades of the New Afrikan Independence Party for their dedication, inspiration, patience and hard-work in advancing Black freedom and self-determination. To learn more about the New Afrikan Independence Party, visit us at www.newafrikan.org . You can also find us on Facebook and Twitter.

All Power to the People!

Free the Land!

Free All Political Prisoners!

Khalid Raheem

March 19, 2019

TABLE OF CONTENTS:

CHAPTER 1

Definitions Shape Our Perspective:

I may as well start here. I have witnessed and participated in numerous debates, discussions and arguments that basically boiled down to conflicting definitions of words, terminology and concepts. How we define our situation and circumstance does indeed shape our perspective and most importantly, influence and determine our response.

To illustrate, an increasing number of Black folks define themselves and others as **'conscious'** and **'woke'**. Some are self-described activist and radicals: while others are labeled as revolutionaries. What do these definitions really mean and how can such clarity help to advance our liberation movement in a practical way?

For example, who and what is the **Black Conscious Community**? How are they defined and what are the requirements for inclusion?

Some folks self-identify as members based on their spiritual beliefs, religious or non-religious beliefs, their diet, personal life-styles: others define themselves according to what videos they have watched, books they have read or workshops attended.

Still, another group cites adherence to certain political philosophies such as Black Nationalism, Pan-Africanism, Cultural Nationalism, Feminism and/or variations of socialist ideology.

In essence, we have a mixture of Black nationalists, Pan-Afrikanists, Kemetics, New Afrikans, atheists, socialists, capitalists, small business owners and entrepreneurs: academics, democrats, republicans, independents, Yoruba, Christians, Hebrews, Moors, Muslims: vegans of differing types and folks of various sexual orientation (LGBTQ) who all lay claim to be members of the **'Black Conscious Community'**.

As such, many serve as self-appointed, or in some instances, duly selected representatives of Black thought, culture and politics.

Many unfamiliar with the various tendencies and nuanced differences between these groups would probably conclude that the Black conscious community was an amorphous unconscious mess.

On and off social media, the conscious community spends an inordinate amount of time and energy attacking and critiquing its members. The vast majority of this criticism is not grounded in principled ideological differences or questions of strategy and tactic.

Most criticism takes on the character of personality conflicts and cultural wars, similar to those waged among and between elements of the ruling-class political parties (democrats, republicans). Many of these cultural wars center on the following issues (in no particular order of importance):

- Black male and female relationships
- Religion versus Spirituality
- Ancient Kemet versus Africa/Afrika
- Black LGBTQ people
- How to deal with non-Black people (especially, but not exclusively white-people)
- Feminism
- Black Celebrity Culture
- Black Nationalist identity versus Class interest (Field Negro versus House Negro)

Additionally, these cultural wars and personality conflicts have created a specialized market for various Black cultural lecturers and their supporters. The fee-for-knowledge circuit has expanded their base of supporters.

Notable cultural lecturers and personalities such as Umar Johnson, Sara Suten Seti, Brother Polight and others travel around the country doing workshops, lectures and selling books and videos promoting their particular vision and version of Black consciousness. Sometimes, even organizing, promoting and staging 'debates' between them.

These spectacles have become akin to a traveling Black Power minstrel show, replete with groupies and followers. They offer lots of information, symbolism and theatrics. However, they have provided very little, if any, strategic leadership or inspiration to the Black community.

More regrettably, many within our communities continue to view these individuals and their movements as genuinely transformative advocates and vehicles for Black freedom and self-determination. However, at this stage of their development, they are not.

The national New Afrikan/Black community is not monolithic and the conscious community reflects that diversity in many ways. However, many within the conscious community are noticeably **apolitical** cultural nationalist, demonstrating a pronounced tendency to avoid both social and political activism.

In other words, you won't find them engaged in much, if any, mass protest or demonstrations even around issues such as affordable housing, police misconduct or racist violence. They would rather talk, text or lecture about it.

The same holds true for political activism in that many will not engage in any form of electoral political struggle, at times being harshly critical of those who do.

On the other hand, there are many sisters and brothers within the conscious community who are very dedicated, focused and disciplined. They continue to put in a tremendous amount of time and energy into actually building real organizations and institutions which promote Black survival, development and self-determination.

You will find them organizing and building feed-the-people programs, health and wellness initiatives, gun and rifle clubs, community-based schools, after-school programs, youth development programs, mental health support groups, etc.

I often say to people that just because you are conscious and woke doesn't make you an activist. Let me explain. A **'Conscious'** or **'Woke'** person is someone who has perhaps become informed regarding the interactions and connections between racism, capitalism, sexism, patriarchy, mass incarceration, health and wellness, etc.

Because of this new found awareness or consciousness, they will initiate a process of self-reflection and introspection, questioning their personal belief systems, values and life-styles. A major part of this personal exploration would involve for example, joining book clubs, conducting individual research and study on various subjects of interest (ancient Afrikan history, civil rights and black power movements, feminism, health and nutrition, etc.), attending workshops and lectures.

The totality of this acute consciousness may result in a commitment to change various aspects of an individual's self-perception and life-style. They may change their diet; embrace a new set of religious and/or spiritual beliefs and practices: change their name, traditional dress, parenting styles or even career choices. This person or group of people are now 'conscious' or 'woke'. They have started a process that hopefully will consist of continued self-examination, education, critical thinking and transformation.

The conscious or 'woke' person will probably share their awareness and corresponding lifestyle with immediate family and friends, particularly those within their household. However, they are not ready to take their newfound awareness or message to the general community or the people. That's the role of an activist.

Activists represent various political persuasions and causes: radical, conservative, liberal, revolutionary: political, environmental, criminal justice, feminist, housing, labor. Activist take their new found awareness and consciousness to the people in order to educate and inspire others for the purpose of making changes within a neighborhood, community, organization and/or system. It's not just enough for them to 'know' about injustice or oppression.

New Afrikan/Black activists organize their families, friends, neighbors and others to actually do something about injustice, oppression and exploitation. They engage in petition-signing campaigns, protest, rallies, and demonstrations: sit-ins, door-to-door outreach, telephone banking, email and twitter blasts, etc.

They also engage in developing programs, projects and institutions to provide immediate and long-term relief, particularly around areas like food, clothing, shelter, education, safety and security. New Afrikan/Black activists are conscious, woke, passionate…and busy.

Conservatives are basically people who want things to remain the same, in favor of the status quo. They want beliefs, values, institutions, structures, systems and power relationships to remain the way they are or have always been.

However, all conservatives are not alike. For example, there are social conservatives, fiscal conservatives as well as political conservatives.

Social conservatives would probably be opposed to supporting gay rights, abortion, same-sex marriage or even basic civil rights for members of the LGBTQ communities. Some social conservatives would also be more likely to oppose any protest during the national anthem or perceived disrespect to the U.S. flag.

As far as social conservatives are concerned, the United States is a Christian nation and should be led by mostly white Christian men (and perhaps a few white women). Social conservatives will on occasion quote the U.S. constitution or their state constitution as a basis for their authority, but utilize the implied moral authority of the Bible and religious writings frequently.

Fiscal conservatives are focused on economic and fiscal issues. Basically, how resources are utilized to make money (economy) and how the money is managed (fiscal). Many state governments today are passing various forms of legislation legalizing the growth, distribution and retail sale of marijuana for recreational use in order to increase state revenue. If they were legally permitted to produce, regulate and tax crack...they would.

They generally support big business, fewer restrictions on multi-national corporations and lower taxes for the super-rich and wealthy: but also cut-backs to social services and entitlements such as welfare, food stamps, social security and Medicare.

They emphasize the importance of balancing the budget (tax revenues should equal expenditures), but are usually okay with spending lots of government monies on the military and the police. They generally balance the state and federal budgets off the backs of the working-class and poor as opposed to increasing taxes on the super-rich and wealthy.

The **political and legal conservatives** focus on the interpretation and application of the U.S. constitution, especially when it comes to the first (1st) and second (2nd) amendments.

Freedoms of speech, freedom of religion, freedom of assembly, the right to bear arms, states' rights are their main areas of engagement. These are the folks who you hear asking "what would the founding fathers do".

They don't seem to consider that when the U.S. constitution was ratified in 1789, native peoples were being murdered for their land, Afrikans were being enslaved for our labor and only white-men who owned property could vote. Four (Washington, Jefferson, Madison, Monroe) of the first five U.S. presidents were all slave-masters from the Virginia aristocracy.

Political and legal conservatives or 'constitutional purist' just can't seem to accept the reality that the 'founding fathers' could not have anticipated that the United States would develop into a 21st century multi-racial, multi-ethnic, multi-religious corporate-capitalist empire. Of course, there are conservatives who fit one or more of the above descriptions. Traditional politics has been known to make very strange bedfellows (alliances, coalitions).

Although most conservatives in the United States are white people, conservatism as an ideology is not restricted by race. There are indeed Black conservatives fitting the above descriptions. You will also find conservatism within both mainstream political parties (Democrats, Republicans); however there is a more pronounced tendency within the Republican Party.

Conservatism is also found within the Black conscious community too. Some woke or conscious folks are socially conservative, but radical in their critique of white-supremacy and the political-economy of the United States. For them, only specific types of Black people are qualified to contribute, participate in or benefit from the movement for Black/New Afrikan freedom. All too often, those qualifications have more to do with gender, sexual orientation and/or religion as opposed to courage, commitment and skill-sets.

Liberals don't want revolution. Liberals tend to favor gradual, incremental reforms or changes to an existing social order and system. Liberalism as a political philosophy favors increased and gradual civil liberties and civil rights, but not a fundamental shift in the relationships of power and control of resources. Hence, here within the United States, we find liberals and progressives who will support calls to end police-brutality, provide affordable housing and defend the voting rights act…but won't support reparations or self-determination for Black people. They will claim that such policies are divisive or that the time is not yet right. In terms of Black freedom, liberalism fosters dependency, not liberation.

Most liberals in the United States are members of the Democratic Party, although you will find them among third or independent political parties as well. Black liberal politicians tend to abhor and dislike genuine radical Black Nationalism, except when it serves their interest to appear militant. Some will make a public display of their loyalty to the Black community by engaging in safe activities such as controlled marches, demonstrations, holiday celebrations and back-to-school activities. These types of activities give the community the impression that this particular politician is okay and really looking out for the interest of the people, when in essence these activities are staged to keep the Black votes coming in for the next election cycle.

The vast majority of Black liberal politicians do not truly fight for the interest of its Black working class and poor constituency either. They sell them out at almost every opportunity. Nowadays, that sellout usually involves taking money and campaign contributions from major corporations and Wall Street operatives via political action committees (PACS). Local political campaigns derive support from their local party establishment and business community. If the area is being targeted for gentrification, real estate developers will also throw some money around.

Take a look at the various cities and areas across the U.S. that are still home to relatively large, but declining, Black populations: for example, Detroit, Chicago, New York, Philadelphia and Washington, D.C. The vast majority have been controlled and managed by the Democratic Party establishment and its liberal wing for decades. In spite of the heroic sacrifices of the civil rights movement and passage of landmark legislation such as the civil rights bill (1964), the voting rights act (1965); the fair housing act (1968) and thousands of Black elected and appointed public officials: working-class and poor Blacks in the U.S. are constantly struggling to survive.

White liberal and so-called progressive groups and organizations are no better. Again, supporting incremental (a little at a time) change, but nothing that is going to fundamentally change the balances of power for Black people or 'rock the boat' on our behalf, especially the working-class and poor.

Neo-liberalism is another version of liberalism. It supports and empowers the status quo and is firmly opposed to New Afrikan/Black freedom and self-determination. Like traditional liberalism, neo-liberalism fosters containment and dependency. What I present is a definition based on some fundamental characteristics.

Neo-liberalism at home manifest itself as a system which remains firmly committed to capitalism and the economic exploitation of all workers, especially those of color. It tolerates the existence of the safety net programs of FDR's New Deal and LBJ's Great Society, but advocates aggressively for their privatization (government services ran by private businesses: for example, schools, prisons, trash/garbage collection, etc.).

It raises the profile of co-opted labor union bureaucrats while suppressing the voice and influence of its rank and file members. Through globalization and automation, many people have lost jobs, union membership has plummeted and more and more workers are being forced to accept unfavorable terms and conditions for continued employment.

Neo- liberalism is an outgrowth of the Democratic Party's successful effort to become more like the Republican Party regarding key aspects of United States fiscal and social policy.

Neo-liberal politicians like Bill Clinton gave us the Crime Bill of 1994 (Violent Crime Control and Law Enforcement Act) and the Welfare Reform Act of 1996 (Personal Responsibility and Work Opportunity Reconciliation Act). Hilary Clinton coined the infamous phrase 'super predator' when describing both the youthful perpetrators and youthful victims of urban violence during the 1990's.

Neo-liberalism enjoys a tremendous amount of support from Wall Street banks and financiers because they want to count on politicians making it as easy as possible for them (banks, finance and investment companies) to make tons of money with as little regulation or opposition as possible. More telling, even now (2019) as various candidates for the 2020 presidential race are making public announcements of their candidacy, several democratic party candidates (Kamala Harris, Corey Booker, Elizabeth Warren) have already been scheduled for vetting by the wealthy elite of Wall Street. They are placing and hedging their bets (i.e., campaign contributions) as to which candidates can best serve their interest. Just like the Clintons, Barack Obama also ascribes to neo-liberalism.

Capitalism today is a world-wide phenomenon always seeking new markets, cheap or relatively inexpensive labor and the development or exploitation of new technologies. It's what most folks refer to as **globalization.**

Nation-states, corporations, businesses and wealthy individuals are all competing for some degree of power either regionally and/or globally. Businesses are not necessarily loyal to the nation-state of their origin and will massively unemploy their fellow citizen/workers in order to increase market share and make more money in another region or country.

So although neo-liberalism is restrictive, conservative and oppressive when it comes to political-economy, it provides a lot of cheap goods (cell phones, computers, sneakers/tennis shoes, clothing) made in other countries by mostly workers of color (Afrikan, Asian, Latinx) who are severely exploited by working extremely long hours in sometimes unsafe environments for relatively little pay.

Neo-liberalism is also noticeably less restrictive regarding cultural/social policy. You can smoke all the weed you want, practice whatever religion or non-religion you please: self-identify to your heart's desire, love anyone you want, marry anyone you want… as long as you don't aspire to overthrow the status quo by dismantling white supremacy and all that comes with it (capitalism, misogyny, patriarchy, imperialism).

Neo-liberalism abroad looks eerily the same no matter which major political party is in office. That's because, for the most part, it is the same. Whether Bush (I, II), Clinton, Obama or Trump, neo-liberal foreign policy requires and mandates the protection of, and if feasible, the expansion of the U.S. empire.

Basically, continued competition with the likes of Russia, China: financial support and strategic direction for the North Atlantic Treaty Organization (NATO), the United Nations (U.N.) and the European Union (with or without the United Kingdom): unconditional support for the apartheid nation-state of Israel: keeping Black and Brown nations in perpetual debt via the World Bank and International Monetary Fund (IMF): economic isolation for socialist or independent nation-states like Venezuela, Cuba, Iran: the continued bombing, droning, and occupation of predominantly Afrikan and/or Muslim people and countries around the world for their natural resources (e.g., oil) and geo-political advantage. For example, the wars in Iraq, Afghanistan and Syria: the U.S. military presence and expansion throughout Africa (AFRICOM), and the numerous undocumented and unconstitutional (not approved by U.S. congress) conflicts worldwide (for example, in Yemen).

Rebels are the people who are non-conformist and challenge traditional ways of thinking, behaving and living. They cause us to question ourselves and the ideas and ideals we so casually embrace and promote. They cause us to question their relevancy and application. Some rebels are extremely anti-authoritarian and reject any notion of authority or accountability except that which is created by them. Most adults in U.S. society experience a period of socialization which involves questioning or rebelling against the norms of one's family, religion or prevailing culture. The majority will transcend this type of rebellion as they mature into adulthood.

Because of the impact of white-supremacy on our families, neighborhoods and communities, we have developed a very distinct rebel class engaged in various degrees and types of rebellion which oftentimes intersect. Socially and economically many would be labeled as working-class, working-poor or low-income, although there are indeed many middle class (or former middle class) participants in this group. Some are creative and/or performing artist. Some are straight up criminals and hustlers. Others are only marginally involved with the traditional ways of feeding and supporting themselves.

Borrowing from the narratives and writings of Frantz Fanon, the Black Panther Party defined some components of this group as the **lumpen-proletariat or 'lumpen' for short**. Unemployed, unemployable, formerly incarcerated and convicted, part-time workers: homeless families, homeless veterans, homeless youth (for example in Allegheny County, Pennsylvania, 40% of the homeless are young people who have aged-out of foster care).

Fast food workers who sell weed (marijuana) in between shifts: public school teachers with graduate degrees who actually live in their car: neighborhood drug-cartels run by aspiring hip-hop artists who use profits to help finance their dreams and pay bills: women and young girls using brains and bodies for survival or being unwilling victims of sex trafficking and exploitation. This is the post-industrial 21st century United States where the federal minimum wage is still just $7.25 per hour and countless people are working multiple jobs, engaging in criminal activities and side hustles just to survive. Where workers float and transition between working-class and lumpen on a regular basis.

These are the rebels. They hustle, get high, commit crimes, reject most established religion, and distrust the system (especially the police). They love their families as well as the neighborhoods, street organizations (gangs) and cliques they represent. They believe in justice (karma and reciprocity) and share the same basic middle-class dreams and fantasy as most Americans (house, car, paid vacation, better future for their children).

However, throughout the course of urban conflict such as rebellions and insurrections as in the aftermath of the Rodney King verdict of 1992 or the response to the police murder of Michael Brown in Ferguson, Missouri in 2014, they continue to demonstrate tremendous courage, bravery and humanity in spite of all their personal and collective flaws. They are acutely in tune with the pulse of neighborhood youth and community sentiment. Particularly in Ferguson, they played a key and crucial role in mobilizing and organizing forces to confront the status quo regarding police murder. Unfortunately, career opportunist in the form of professional activists like Black Lives Matter and others from the non-profit industrial complex would soon converge on Ferguson, misdirect, co-opt and marginalize the leadership and authenticity of the rebels and establish themselves (Black Lives Matter, etc.) as the official spokespersons and representatives of the movement.

The issue with the **Rebel Class** is that those involved in street crime and hustling have developed predatory gangster mentalities and lifestyles that don't serve the long-term collective best interest of Black/New Afrikan people. It contributes to serious damage to the Black family and Black social fabric. Their rejection of traditional American values and behaviors and their militant opposition to police violence shouldn't be misinterpreted as wholesale support or endorsement for radical or revolutionary change. Much personal transformation and political education needs to take place beforehand. Prisons are full of Black/New Afrikan rebels, but the vast majorities have not developed into radicals or revolutionaries such as Malcolm X or George Jackson.

Besides the predatory behavior of certain elements within the rebel class, they have a tendency to be undisciplined, overly materialistic and obsessed with social image over social substance. All of which makes them ripe and primary candidates for recruitment by the counter-revolutionary forces of the state (as informants and agent-provocateurs) via operations such as COINTELPRO and the recently disclosed FBI Black Identity Extremist initiative. It also makes them extremely vulnerable to the manipulations, cooptation and exploitation by the professional organizers of the non-profit industrial complex and liberal-wing of the Democratic Party.

Their street credibility and reputation are often used by these representatives of white-supremacy (non-profit industrial complex, liberals, progressives, politicians) to maintain control over the hearts and minds of the Black/New Afrikan community, particularly our youth. This is accomplished by promoting either passivity (non-violence): feeble responses to injustice (staged marches, rallies, prayer circles, doves, balloons, music concerts) and/or continued faith in the systems' ability to correct itself by convening hearings, commissions or proposing legislation.

Reminds one of how, during the urban riots/rebellions of the 1960's, 'the white-man' would call upon the Black church ministers and Black celebrities to go throughout the 'ghetto' and encourage Black youth to 'be cool'.

Nevertheless, rebels are full of potential for genuine personal transformation and positive impact on New Afrikan/Black communities. I know of many formerly incarcerated people and former gang-members who are dedicated to improving the lives of Black people and others. For some the transformation has been both radical and revolutionary.

We have elements within our communities who understand the necessity of thorough and complete systemic change in order for New Afrikan/Black people to be truly free. They are dedicated and committed people who clearly recognize the root causes of Black/New Afrikan oppression and demand its eradication as a necessity for our freedom and self/group-determination. However, they often perceive victory and liberation as the culmination of a series of events instead of a process. These are the **Radicals**. They want revolutionary change today, this very minute and believe it is just around the corner.

They echo the philosophy of "if all Black people would just...,." (Select those that apply. This list is not exhaustive):

- All Come Together!
- Stop Voting!
- Arm Ourselves and Fight Back!
- Vote In Every Election!
- Support Black Business!
- Attend the Big March!
- Do For Self!
- Read More!
- Follow a Specific Leader!

They seek immediate and permanent relief from white-supremacy and economic injustice (capitalism, imperialism, self and group hatred) without having yet developed a strategic understanding of how to actually obtain victory or rebuild/create a new people and new society. One of the characteristics of an **undeveloped Radical** is the tendency to lose faith in the movement, lose his or her self-confidence and give in to hopelessness and despair. Once again, we must emphasize the importance of political education and organizational development in the pursuit of Black freedom and self/group determination. Revolutionary struggle and victory is a process, not a singular or series of events.

Those within the Black/New Afrikan community who desire and advocate for a comprehensive change in the conditions of our lives and who work to challenge, overthrow and remove the existing white-supremacist yoke of oppression from the throats of Black people are **Revolutionaries**.

They demand **Freedom and Power** and clearly understand that Black people can't really have one without the other. Revolutionaries are not just against racism, but are anti-capitalist and anti-imperialist as well.

And, just like the national Black/New Afrikan community, the **Black Revolutionary Class** is not monolithic in its political perspectives and ideologies. We continue to wage ideological struggle concerning misogyny, patriarchy, feminism and the role of LGBTQ issues within the broader context of the movement. We also have conflicting visions for what this new society should look like as well as strategic and tactical disagreements on how best to get there. However, the **Black Revolutionary Class** is firmly committed to the dismantling and destruction of white-supremacy.

Hence, Black Revolutionaries don't belong to either of the mainstream political parties. Black revolutionaries are not Democrats. Black revolutionaries are not Republicans. They are not members of any political party which supports and defends capitalist exploitation at home and imperialism and militarism throughout the world.

The Black Revolutionary Class falls along the ideological spectrum of Black Nationalism - Pan-Afrikanism – Socialism – Communism - Feminism – Womanism – Environmentalism – Internationalism - Anarchism and various religious, spiritual and cultural tendencies.

The Black Revolutionary Class is composed of **Black Radical and Revolutionary Activists** who are engaged in multiple or specific areas of movement building and struggle such as education, creative and performing arts, housing, criminal justice, political prisoners, electoral politics, economic development, labor organizing, self and group defense, etc. They read, study, observe, organize and teach. They are strategic and combine theory with practice.

There is general agreement throughout the national Black/New Afrikan community as to what constitute some of the more serious challenges facing it, especially among working-class and low-income members. For example: racism, unemployment, homelessness, education, mass incarceration, poverty, police violence, gentrification, voter suppression, community violence. There is also general agreement regarding the impacts these conditions have had on the quality of New Afrikan/Black life as well: race-based income and wealth disparities, education gaps between Black students versus non-Black students: hypertension/high blood-pressure, substance-abuse, mental health problems: broken families, vulnerable neighborhoods and communities (public safety, food and water security, gentrification).

Some people may not yet have developed a perspective as to what they are actually fighting for. Are we fighting for civil rights or human rights? Maybe a continuum which involves some of both. Nowadays, we have all types and varieties of liberals and progressives claiming to be against white-supremacy, racism and injustice.

Many have come to identify Donald Trump and his presidency as their center of focus and organized resistance. So, what happens if Trump and his administration are removed through impeachment or he (Trump) loses his presidential bid for re-election in 2020: Is that the victory we've all been fighting for? Have the structures, institutions and systems (power) of white-supremacy and economic injustice been dismantled?

Donald Trump is not an aberration or distortion of race, class and gender relations in America. He is just representative of another version. I contend that much of the activism among today's liberals and progressives is basically:

1. A reaction to Bernie Sanders and his supporters being snubbed by the Democratic Party establishment in favor of Hilary Clinton.
2. A reaction to Donald Trump's surprise and upset victory over pro-Wall Street, pro-war candidate Hilary Clinton.

Draped in the covering of righteous indignation, liberal philanthropy, a new found identity of 'democratic socialist', and the co-opted networks and energies from the Black Lives Matter movement (M4BL), **the liberal, progressive wing** of the Democratic Party is pushing hard to present themselves as the natural protectors and allies of the Black/New Afrikan community.

The neo-liberal and more moderate wing of the Democratic Party are doing the same, although by different methods. They are utilizing traditional civil-rights leadership networks and the old-school Black civil-rights icons such as Congressman John Lewis to promote their agenda.

Both factions separately and jointly are fighting to replace Donald Trump as President of the United States, maintain a Democratic Party majority in the

U.S. House of Representatives and hopefully gain a Democratic Party majority in the U.S. Senate. All factions are also working hard to maintain and expand their political base of support within the New Afrikan/Black community while simultaneously (and carefully) attempting to regain many of those white voters (democrats and independents) who voted for Trump in 2016. To this end, the Democratic Party has been heavily involved in the recruitment and funding of Black people (particularly, Black women) to run for local and statewide public office.

On the other hand, factions within the Republican party are enjoying their control of the White House, Senate and U.S. Supreme Court even as they struggle with some of the challenges posed by Trumps personal history, campaign allegations, policy initiatives and leadership style. Both Republicans and Democrats see themselves as the best qualified representatives, custodians and defenders of the American empire.

So, as Black/New Afrikans involved in all sorts of activism ranging from anti-police brutality to environmental justice to routine survival, the questions remain: **What are we fighting for? What is our agenda? What is our end-game?**

In conclusion, we know that people can be awoke and conscious and not necessarily be activist. We know that there are all types of activist who focus or concentrate their passion, skills and energies in multiple areas of movement building and struggle. We realize that among Black/New Afrikan activists, that not all activism is radical or revolutionary in purpose or intent.

Much of today's' activism is actually **Reformist** and is not intended to create a fundamentally different society which liberates and empowers Black people. It is only intended to correct the most blatant expressions of injustice, while maintaining the continued racial and economic oppression and exploitation of the national Black/New Afrikan community. We know that liberals, neo-liberals and progressives within the non-profit industrial complex work in collusion with (mostly) Democratic Party operatives to control the narrative and movement building activities among disgruntled members of the Black community, especially the youth.

We know that those who are mostly living on the edge as chronically unemployed, underemployed, homeless, currently or formerly incarcerated, hustlers, gang-members and petty criminals constitute what the Black Panther Party via Fanon described as the 'lumpen' or those we define as rebels. The rebel class has some admirable qualities, but many counter-revolutionary tendencies and challenges that must be addressed.

We know that real Black revolutionaries are not members of any political party which is grounded, rooted in or supports white-supremacy and economic injustice, whether at home or abroad. We know that radical thinking, analysis and action is a key component to becoming revolutionary. Striving to understand the root and fundamental causes, structures, institutions and systems of our oppression is crucial to obtaining victory over it.

We know that revolutionaries engage in some type of scientific process (study, research, action, evaluation). They try to be strategic, not reactionary. They understand that revolution is a process and not an event. They constantly struggle in sustaining and maintaining a life-long commitment. The Black Revolutionary Class is not monolithic and comprises people of differing ideological perspectives. They also represent numerous religious, spiritual and cultural tendencies and varying degrees of experience.

We realize that both mainstream political parties (Democrats, Republicans) actually represent competing segments within the ruling-class elite of the United States. Neither party represents the collective best interest of New Afrikan/Black people, especially those who are working class and low-income. We realize that the Trump presidency and white house is an enemy, but not the enemy...,

Hopefully, the definitions listed above will **<u>provoke some discussion and debate</u>** among various groups and cadre. We hope such exchanges will improve our overall strategic understandings and sharpen our daily practice.

CHAPTER 2

Why An Independent Black Political Party

In the 1950's there were just a few hundred Black elected or appointed officials throughout the United States. In 1965 we had several hundred resulting from the passage of civil rights legislation. Today we have thousands and still no justice, nor freedom for the national Black community.

For the last fifty years, the Black community has consistently and almost exclusively been members of the Democratic Party. We have consistently supported and voted for Democratic Party candidates nationwide in the process. Democrats have been able to count on the Black/New Afrikan vote for all local, statewide and national elections.

What do we have to show for over 50 years of such solid loyalty? To date: one Black president (Barack Obama) who while a staunch international defender of the American empire (ISIS, drones, immigrant detentions, AFRICOM) and the rights of various marginalized groups within the U.S., projected timidity and trepidation when it came to advocating for any substantial targeted relief or remedies for Black people. It appeared that he, Obama was almost afraid to be too closely associated or aligned with any sort of 'Black Agenda', although he received well over 90% of the Black vote during both of his presidential runs.

Many of us, radicals and revolutionaries alike, were patiently waiting for some display of executive presidential power regarding relief from the escalating vigilante and police murder of Black people (Trayvon Martin, Michael Brown). Instead we got occasional public reprimands and rebukes concerning dysfunctional aspects of Black culture and family life.

Looking for serious help in response to the financial collapse of 2008, aspiring Black/New

Afrikan working-class and middle-class families saw their personal savings, investments and housing-equity vanish. On the other hand, Wall Street banks and finance companies were massively bailed out. Neo-Liberalism prevailed and the Occupy Wall Street Movement was born. 'Yes We Can' quickly became No He Didn't.

Unfortunately, even today, many Blacks/New Afrikans remained obsessed with Barack Obama's **presidential style** while ignoring his historic lack of **presidential substance** concerning the interest of the national Black community.

Black people are disproportionately represented in almost every **negative demographic** imaginable: poverty, education, unemployment, income inequality, net worth or wealth: life expectancy, infant mortality, death while giving birth: incarceration, parole/probation, homicide, victims of hate crime, being killed or brutalized by police: homelessness, hypertension/high-blood pressure, on and on. In other words, we are usually at the bottom or close to it in every conceivable category concerning the quality of human life here within the United States.

You will find these conditions dominant throughout just about every major city and/or metropolitan area within the United States with any substantial, albeit declining or displaced, Black populations. For example, places such as New York, Philadelphia, Pittsburgh, Cleveland, Los Angeles, Detroit, Chicago, Milwaukee, Atlanta, Houston, Newark, Washington, D.C. and Baltimore. The other thing you find is that the vast majority of these cities and areas have been run, not by Republicans, but by the elected and appointed officials of the Democratic Party. They have held sway over politics and the quality of Black life in these locations, in some instances, for the last 30-50 years or more. In response to the gains and advancements made by the Civil Rights Movement (CRM) and the cooptation of certain elements within the Black Power Movement (BPM), the race and gender of politicians and officials have alternated, but the liberal and neo-liberal policies of Black oppression and containment have remained constant.

The face of neo-colonial politics and control within the Black/New Afrikan community is the Democratic Party. Until recently, those faces have been mainly white and male with variations of Black, Brown and/or Asian folks as representatives. For example, out of all the cities listed above, Pittsburgh, Pennsylvania is the only city that has never had a Black/New Afrikan person as mayor.

Pittsburgh has however, had a Jewish woman, Sophie Masloff as mayor.

Nationally, today's garden variety of overseers includes women, members of the LGBTQ community, Indigenous/Native Americans and Muslims. Neo-colonial diversity orchestrated by either democrats or republicans should not be construed as an example of radical popular democracy. This is definitely not what democracy looks like.

In terms of political representation, Blacks/New Afrikans experienced some of our largest and most significant achievements during the periods immediately after the U.S. civil war or Reconstruction. Blacks were elected to all levels of government office, including sheriff, mayor, governor, senator, congressman. Even this progress was severely tainted by laws at the time which did not permit women to vote or hold office. The betrayals of the Republican Party and violent backlash from white-supremacist and white-terrorist groups ultimately decimated these political gains as the forces of the former Confederate States of America (CSA) were able to regroup and establish the system which came to be known as 'Jim Crow'.

The U.S. Senate is the most powerful legislative body in the country. There are 100 members.

Currently in 2019, there are only three (3) Black U.S. senators. The U.S. House of Representatives is now much more representative numerically of the Black population, having 52 Black members out of the 435 representatives. However, there are currently no Black/New Afrikan governors.

The Congressional Black Caucus (CBC) is supposed to advocate for and introduce legislation on behalf of so-called African American people, but spends a lot of time socializing, entertaining corporate lobbyist and campaigning for re-election. Instead of pushing radical proposals for relief from the oppression of white-supremacy, the CBC delivers style over substance. They too, are complicit in perpetuating the system of neo-colonial control over Black/New Afrikan communities.

Our national Black community would benefit substantially from **proportional political representation** based on our numerical population demographics. For example, since Blacks/New Afrikans are anywhere from 13-15% of the national population, we should be guaranteed at least 13-15% of all seats in the U.S. Senate, House of Representatives and Governorships. That would translate into 13-15 U.S. Senators, 57-65 House Representatives and 7-8 State Governors. This formula should also be applied to federal court appointments as well. These types of changes could result in serious and substantive relief for Blacks/New Afrikans throughout the United States.

The call and movement for **Reparations** is yet another area where the Congressional Black Caucus (CBC) and local and statewide Black/New Afrikan public officials could play a serious role if indeed they decide to be more than just neo-colonial puppets and overseers.

Recently, several candidates vying for the presidential nomination of the Democratic Party in 2020 have made or issued some type of statement regarding their support for Reparations. I believe most, if not all of this chatter, is no more than a feeble attempt to pander to the Black/New Afrikan vote and isolate 2016 and 2020 candidate Bernie Sanders from emerging as a potential majority choice within the Black community. To date, Sanders has stated emphatically his opposition to reparations, echoing his statements from his 2016 presidential run and labeling reparations divisive. Instead, he advocates some type of economic plan to improve the conditions of all Americans, but especially Blacks/New Afrikans.

More liberal, progressive non-sense when it comes to Black people. However, he (Sanders) continues to support U.S. foreign aid to Israel and reparations being paid to Israel by Germany and others because of the Jewish holocaust. Go figure.

To be clear: there are some politicians and public officials who mean well and are sincere in their effort to represent the people within their district. But, the institution and system of American politics itself is fraught with corruption, dishonesty and driven by white-supremacy and economic injustice. Both the republicans and democrats have clearly shown that to be the case.

We must organize, develop and support our own independent political parties and vehicles for electoral struggle and the acquisition of political power. We must stop giving our political capital (endorsements and votes) away to people that clearly do not share our short-term nor long-term collective best interest. We must clearly come to understand the difference between political symbolisms versus political substance.

We must never allow ourselves to be manipulated and rendered impotent by Black (or other) politicians running around masquerading as friends and protectors of the Black/New Afrikan community while they sell-out our homes, neighborhoods, schools, children, elders and future. We need independent Black/New Afrikan politics that is radical, revolutionary and relevant. Political

Parties Do Matter. Get the Elephant Out of Your Room. Get Down From That Donkey. Join the Panthers..,

CHAPTER 3

Black Lives Matter (BLM) Is NOT the Black Liberation Movement (BLM)

Bursting on the scene approximately five years ago in response to the increasing vigilante and police violence against Black/New Afrikan people, Black Lives Matter has developed into an important and significant network and movement in addressing the specifics of Black oppression. It has done much to raise awareness, mobilize and organize people in its efforts at pursuing justice and creating safe spaces particularly for Black/New Afrikan youth and young adults of the LGBTQ community. Its founders and leaders have been recognized far and wide for their groundbreaking work and success at highlighting the importance of justice for Black people within the United States and around the world.

Unfortunately, Black Lives Matter has also engaged in career opportunism by high jacking the energies and organizing of the militant working-class, lumpen and organic leadership emerging out of the police murder of Michael Brown which ignited the Ferguson rebellion of 2014. However, Black Lives Matter was certainly not alone in practicing this type of exploitation and opportunism. There were several other organizations and individuals, including academics that pounced on the intense life and death struggles of Ferguson to carve out or expand some sort of activist or career niche for them. Almost overnight: books were written, documentaries produced, speaking engagements were scheduled and paid for…even as people were still fighting, protesting and being arrested. No shame in their game.

Furthermore Black Lives Matters' cozy and established relationship with the neo-liberal philanthropic community and non-profit industrial complex appears to raise other questions concerning its sense of movement accountability. For example, a previously considered (and highly publicized) 100 million dollar grant via the Ford Foundation.

Lastly, the implicit cooperation (via town hall meetings, voter education and registration drives) with elements within the Democratic Party during recent election cycles such as the mid-term elections and the upcoming 2020 presidential campaigns. Perhaps this represents a tactical alliance among those forces that are centering their political energies on the ouster of Trump from the White House. We will see.

Political pundits, media and liberal activist circles initially labeled Black Lives Matter as the 'new Civil Rights Movement', a label which it (BLM) emphatically rejects. Other more radical and leftist analysts and activists have drawn parallels between Black Lives Matter and the Black Panther Party, concluding that today's **Black Lives Matter Movement (M4BL)** is the modern day **Black Liberation Movement.**

While the Black Panther Party was one of the leading organizations within the Black Liberation Movement, it was only one among several including the Nation of Islam, Congress of Afrikan People, Republic of New Afrika, Black Liberation Army and a host of various local, statewide and national organizations fighting for some version of Black freedom and independence. All these versions included demands for reparations and self-determination. Most, if not all, also called for the convening of a national plebiscite (vote) to be held among Black people. The plebiscite would concern our current and future relationship with the United States. Some called for this plebiscite to be supervised by the United Nations.

Others such as the Black Panther Party actually moved in the direction of convening delegates to engage in the process of declaring independence and writing a new U.S. constitution, for example the Revolutionary Peoples Constitutional Convention held in Philadelphia in 1970. The Congress of Afrikan Peoples (CAP) was convening and making similar declarations in places such as Atlanta during this period as well. CAP was also transitioning into a Marxist-Leninist-Maoist ideologically based organization. The Republic of New Afrika had preceded both in 1968 by stating its call for an independent Black (New Afrikan) nation-state to be based in the areas of the south where there were majority Black/New Afrikan populations.

And of course, the Nation of Islam (NOI) under the leadership of Elijah Muhammad and articulated through his representatives Malcolm X and later, Minister Farrakhan had consistently called for some degree of Black freedom and autonomy, preferably concentrating this desired economic and political power in the southern United States. The NOI had been advocating and pushing the message of Black self-determination since the 1930's.

These and similar types of groups, organizations and individuals comprised the Black Liberation Movement. They were all essentially Black Nationalist formations with varying degrees of Pan-

Africanist and Internationalist perspective, which eventually developed and transitioned their ideologies into the following tendencies:

- **Black Panther Party:** (Revolutionary Nationalism/Inter-communalism)
- **Nation of Islam:** (Militant Religious and Bourgeois Nationalism: Territorial Nationalism)
- **Congress of Afrikan Peoples:** (Cultural Nationalism/Marxism-Leninism-Maoism)
- **Republic of New Afrika:** (Territorial/Revolutionary Nationalism)
- **Black Liberation Army:** (As an armed force, multiple-tendencies were represented, including Anarchism)

They not only demanded social and economic justice for Black people, they challenged the state for power in pursuit of such justice. They came to understand the connection between freedom and power and that Blacks/New Afrikans can't realistically enjoy one without having the other. Internally they consciously (and sometimes reluctantly) struggled around issues of sexism, patriarchy, chauvinism, religion, culture, and class exploitation.

Furthermore, during its development, the Black Panther Party acknowledged the need and importance of consciously and specifically addressing oppression and exploitation based on sexual preference and orientation. They called upon all revolutionaries to recognize, unite with and work to eradicate the significant oppression experienced by members of the LGBTQ community.

Is the **Black Lives Matter** network and movement a revolutionary initiative? Has it or does it currently challenge the systems, structures and institutions of white-supremacy and economic injustice for power? Social justice reform is not enough.

Or is it merely a construction set up to amplify the most egregious examples of injustice while muffling and controlling the activities and narrative of the oppressed and marginalized within our communities?

Is its ideological grounding and base in radical LGBTQ Nationalism broad enough and deep enough to provide a practical launching pad for non-LGBTQ members of the Black/New Afrikan community who engage in revolutionary movement-building and struggle?

Does BLM enjoy a broad and solid base of support or are its messaging and numbers just basically a reflection of generous financial support from liberal philanthropists and the non-profit industrial complex?

And what is the updated status of the several people who were arrested, convicted and sentenced to prison (political prisoners) as a result of their actual or alleged participation in the Ferguson rebellion? Do they receive support from the Black Lives Matter network or movement?

What about the numerous grassroots activists from the area (St. Louis County) who have been killed or found dead under questionable circumstances in the last few years? Has BLM used its resources and/or media clout to highlight these situations: perhaps demanding investigations or outside intervention?

Is the leadership of Black Lives Matter (Network & M4BL) composed of working class and poor Blacks or mostly non-profit professionals and academics? If there were no funding available and the cameras were turned off, would there still be people available and committed to do the work? An individual's socio-economic (class) relationship to the system (white-supremacy and economic injustice) does matter. Dedicated and revolutionary Black leadership matters too.

CHAPTER 4

The Limitations of Black Nationalism, Cultural Nationalism and Pan-Afrikanism

One of the first initial responses to racism and white supremacy is to look for help and assistance, particularly from amongst those with whom you may share common characteristics and/or circumstances. In other words, we will look around and seek out other Black people for help. Ever since the initial conditions of our capture and enslavement, Blacks/New Afrikans have been seeking ways to communicate with one another and organize so as to help one another deal with the violence, exploitation and oppression associated with white-supremacy and racialized slavery, capitalism, colonialism and imperialism.

In spite of initial differences in ethnicity, language, customs and religion, we as descendants of enslaved and colonized Afrikans have been shaped and molded into a unique socio-politico entity here within the United States. That transformation is not stagnant, but continues to evolve as we include and embrace even more Afrikan-descended diversity into our ranks.

For example, there is currently vigorous debate occurring among Blacks within the United States concerning the status of those Blacks who are not descendants of those enslaved here within the U.S. Should they be entitled to enjoy the benefits derived from the struggles waged for American civil rights? What about Reparations? Should the more recently arrived Sisters and Brothers be included in the discussion and if yes, how so, and to what extent? Are they even entitled to speak for and/or represent the history, legacy and continuing struggle of Blacks/New Afrikans?

Do they identify themselves as 'African-American', Black, New Afrikan or do they prefer Nigerian-American, Haitian-American, etc. And, what does all this mean in terms of mobilizing and organizing the forces and power of Black people in advancing a revolutionary 21st century agenda for liberation.

In addition to the multitude of philosophical, political and very real social challenges faced by our national community, this has taken center stage for some folks. Descendants of U.S. Slaves (DOS) versus Non-Descendants of U.S. Slaves (NON-DOS). One more addition to the numerous and contentious topics debated on social media like a Black Power Minstrel Hour.

Many folks outside the experience of Black oppression and even some of us, who are intricately a part of it, fail to recognize the oppression of Black/New Afrikan people as a **collective phenomenon**. It is so much more comfortable to believe that the gross wealth and income inequalities between Blacks and whites are due to Black folks just being lazy. Or that there are so many Blacks in prison because we are inherently (naturally) inclined toward criminal activity. Never mind the decades and generations of slavery, Jim Crow, poverty, state-protected (KKK) and state-generated (police) terror directed against Black people.

It rattles the psyche of many whites to accept the historic reality that Blacks in the United States have been **collectively targeted** for race-based systemic and institutional oppression and exploitation. It doesn't reconcile with the standard sanitized versions of U.S. history that the majority of us have been spoon-fed.

It's very difficult to reconcile admiration, love and respect for the founding fathers (and mothers): writers of the U.S. Constitution, signers of the Declaration of Independence when you later learn that, indeed many were slaveholders who raped and molested Black girls, boys, men and women: fathered numerous Black children, separated families and sold Black people like we were chickens and livestock, including some of their own children. They were the original dead-beat dads (and moms) of the United States.

The historical forces which impacted our development have basically been capture, enslavement, resistance and survival. Our **resistance** has taken on various forms during the last several centuries from:

Rebellion (Cinque, Nat Turner):

Repatriation back to Africa (Emigration Movement):

Establishing independent and armed settlements (Maroons): singularly or in cooperation with Indigenous people and/or indentured and marginalized whites

Escape to free or neutral territory: often with the assistance of allies and friends (for example, Abolitionist Movement and the Underground Railroad).

Economically, socially and politically, our **survival** has taken on various expressions, forms and ideals ranging from **voluntary separation** to **radical integration**. Because of the unique experience of enslavement and the perpetual collective exploitation and oppression based primarily on race, Blacks/New Afrikans now constitute a specific economic, cultural, social and political entity within the United States.

For example, I earlier commented on how Black people dominate almost every negative indicator concerning the quality of life among people living within the U.S. such as income, wealth, life expectancy, etc. The majority of Black/New Afrikans have roots throughout the southern United States. Many others have roots in the Caribbean Islands and elsewhere as well. As a matter of fact, most Blacks/New Afrikans still live 'down south'. Some live in cities and towns where the overwhelming majority of its residents are Black. We are indeed a **nation-within-a nation** trapped within the confines of a perpetual system of white-supremacy and economic injustice. Blacks/New Afrikans are widely distributed throughout the United States, but we are materially, historically, culturally and contemporaneously grounded and rooted in the southern U.S.

The description above lays the basis and foundation for the development of a Black Nationalist orientation and in some instances, a very deliberate and conscious identification with Black Nationalism as our political, economic and social philosophy.

Historically, the call and response of Black Nationalism has been for the creation, support and control of those institutions and individuals that benefit from and/or supposedly serve the interest of the Black community. Stores, businesses, politicians, schools, police, cultural centers, etc. would all meet these criteria as targets for the implementation of some sort of Black Nationalist or Black Power agenda. Making demands for fundamental or increased Black/New Afrikan representation and authority in areas like government, business, education, arts, public safety and security has been and continues to be a central theme in pursuit of reforms that can deliver measured relief from the ravages of white-supremacy and economic injustice.

What we have discovered is that the forces of white-supremacy have cleverly co-opted and misappropriated both the imagery and substance of demands for any sort of Black Power by identifying, selecting and/or promoting particular types of Black representatives or leaders. Namely, those leaders that don't pose any serious threats or danger to the existence of white-supremacy and economic injustice.

This is accomplished through a conscious and deliberate collusion of forces such as network media, big business/Wall Street, educational institutions, cultural centers and non-profits. However the biggest player and by far the most influential has been and continues to be the two mainstream political parties, especially the Democrats. Vetting, selecting and strategically placing particular types of Black or liberal/neo-liberal leadership among Blacks/New Afrikans has developed into both an art and science for the Democrats.

High-jacking the **Message and Movement** is characteristic of these ploys as well. A recent example is the 'New Green Deal', which originated with Green Party activists but is now being claimed as part of the progressive democrat agenda.

Another example would be the several Democratic Party 2020 presidential candidates publicly expressing some degree of interest in or support for Reparations: a movement that originated with former slaves, their immediate families and descendants and groups like the National Coalition of Blacks for Reparations in America (NCOBRA).

I once had the experience of witnessing folks conduct a rally invoking the name of Assata Shakur. They were chanting Assatas' "it is our duty to fight..." mantra during a 2016 presidential campaign gathering. The candidate they were calling upon us to support was Hilary Clinton. Or maybe it was a Bernie Sanders rally. (This is even more problematic, since Sanders also supported Assata Shakur being placed on the FBI Most Wanted List with a bounty attached and her conditional diplomatic extradition from Cuba).

In either case, I gently reminded someone close by that Assata was not a member of the Democratic Party, but rather had been a member of the Black Panther Party and the Black Liberation Army. Their response was the dumb look.

Promoting style over substance is another key component of neo-colonial deception. For example, our political representatives may be weak, ineffectual and corrupt but **at least they are:**

- Black/New Afrikan (and/or: take your pick…)
- POC (People of Color)
- Not Republican
- Progressive
- Women
- Men
- Heterosexual
- LGBTQ
- Christian
- Muslim
- Afro-Centric
- Well Dressed

- Great Speakers
- Rich
- Well Educated
- Good Athletes

Bill Clinton was dubbed as Americas' 'first Black president' because he spoke the southern Black/New Afrikan dialect well, moved easily around Black folk: was a jazz enthusiast who knew how to play and flow with a saxophone. He appointed a historic number of Blacks/New Afrikans to his cabinet as well.

Barack Obama claimed Chicago as his political home, had an attractive Black family, 'strolled' across the stage before taking the podium: and could play a decent game of basketball. He was also a fan favorite of college hoops (basketball). He also appointed a significant number of Blacks/New Afrikans to his cabinet too.

Clinton gave us double-down mass incarceration (crime bill) and increased hardship for those receiving public assistance (welfare reform act). Obama gave us increased drones, military presence in Africa (via AFRICOM), the destabilization of Libya and assassination of Muamar Gadhafi and very little of value to Black people. Both Clinton and Obama had style.

Blacks/New Afrikans enthusiastically supported both presidents for the duration of their presidential terms in office, a total of sixteen (16) years. No collective **quid pro quo** here. We squandered and wasted our political capital.

Hence, the tendency of Black Nationalist thinking to cloud our political and economic choices by giving cover to **agents and elements of exploitation and neo-colonialism** who are using their so-called 'Blackness' and personal histories as tools for controlling and containing any expression for genuine freedom and liberation. They don't want collective freedom and liberation for our people. Their desire is to remain in political and corporate offices (including colleges and universities) in order to prosper from the intermediary or go-between position they have with the forces of white supremacy and the Black community.

They want to continue to serve as the **'Head Nigger In Charge'** (**HNIC**) over the wants and aspirations of Black people, particularly the working class, poor and lumpen. Why? Because, the working-class, poor and lumpen are the **majority** within the national Black/New Afrikan community. They comprise the group most likely to rebel and seriously challenge the system for power.

Black Nationalism glosses over and clouds our critique of Black economic, social and cultural elites as well. We are conditioned to incessantly worship and imitate all types of greedy, selfish athletes, entertainers and business people just because they are Black and have achieved some degree of personal financial or career success. In the overwhelming majority of cases, their personal success has not done anything to benefit the collective Black community, nor was it ever intended to. We must reject this type of thinking and worthless adoration.

However, we must support and stand with those artist, athletes and entertainers who publicly oppose racism and white-supremacy, particularly those who take a stance (or knell) in support of others and not just because of some sort of personal injury or experience.

Much of what is produced and distributed as mass popular culture (music, film, television) is not only toxic to the continued survival of Black/New Afrikan people, but counter to our collective spiritual, political and socio-economic development. Self and group hatred, gangsterism, misogyny, patriarchy, gratuitous violence, mindless consumerism, waste, exploitation of youth and disregard of elders are indeed counterproductive and counter-revolutionary by- products of this modern-day form of idolatry.

We must vigilantly oppose and guard against reactionary forms of Black Nationalism which teach us to hate and despise people **just because** of their skin color or amount of melanin displayed. It prevents us from recognizing the humanity and goodness among those outside of our tribe/nation and makes it difficult to form and build friendships and mutually beneficial alliances with other oppressed and exploited segments within the American empire.

Reactionary or juvenile forms of Black Nationalism represent the basic and fundamentally visceral response to the reality of living in such an intensely racialized and violent United States. It's a reaction to not just perhaps the personal experience of such violence, but bearing witness to how deeply pervasive and entrenched it is throughout the society you live in. It's what moved Elijah Muhammad, Malcolm X and hundreds of thousands of others then and now to conclude that white people were actually devils: children and operatives of the Devil Himself (Lucifer, Satan, Iblis, Shai'tan).

How else could one rationalize the pervasive and systemic hatred directed towards Blacks and the violence (physical, psychological, social) that accompanies it? For many of us, this (reactionary-juvenile nationalist phase) is a period of enlightenment, research and study. It is painfully excruciating yet necessary if we are to develop politically and socially as radicals and revolutionaries.

As we continue to study, research and work for revolutionary change, we counter the reactionary-juvenile black nationalist narrative with the history of the Abolitionist Movement, John Brown, International Workers of the World (Wobblies), Students for a Democratic Society (SDS), Freedom Summer, Freedom Riders, Rev. James Reeb, Viola Liuzzo, Schwerner, Goodman & Chaney, Linda Evans, Marilyn Buck, David Gilbert and countless other white people, and those with less visible melanin, who have continued to fight hard, not just for the civil and human rights of Black people, but for all people and the planet.

I am thankful for them and the many, mostly white youth who show up to protest against the police murder of Black/New Afrikan people or the disproportionate number of Blacks in prison or the environmental racism impacting our communities where dumpsters multiply and the garbage piles up or the forced displacement, migration from and emptying-out of historic Black neighborhoods due to gentrification (sometimes forcing these same youth to question their families and peers about the housing choices they have made and why).

I also understand that they are present not just as supporters, but as allies who have skin (perhaps, not as dark as mine) in the game too. I realize that capitalism and its latest version of political economy (neo-liberalism) have failed them too.

If they come from low-income and working-class backgrounds, they are either unemployed, underemployed or working at low-paying and menial jobs. If they are college and university students, they are probably facing tremendous debt in order to acquire education that may or may not provide them with the necessary inroads to the jobs needed for their survival and repayment of student debt. If they live within the post-industrial **Rust Belt** area, they probably have family members and/or friends who are victims of the current opioid (drug) crisis that has killed thousands in the last few years. Many whites are now acutely aware of the unfairness of the criminal justice system, because they are now personally impacted by it with growing numbers of citizens and residents having arrest records and under some type of criminal supervision (probation, parole).

So while we continue to work hard, pushing the agenda of Black/New Afrikan self-determination and Reparations, we reject reactionary and juvenile forms of Black Nationalism. We will **work** with those and **support** those and **align** with those who demonstrate the willingness to do the same toward us.

We know that the issues and challenges around racism, white-supremacy and chauvinism will not disappear or wither away. Those challenges to principled unity and mutual respect will continue to need resolution.

Socio-economic systems based on Socialism, Communism, Islam, Christianity, etc. will not, in itself, miraculously eradicate racism or racist ideation. That is ideological fiction and fantasy. Just as Blacks (and other people of color) have been brainwashed to believe in our inherent inferiority, whites (and others) have likewise been brainwashed to believe in their inherent superiority. Like any relationship involving people, building alliances and/or coalitions requires work.

Culture is basically defined as the way in which people live. How we live is determined by a multitude of factors such as climate, available technologies, material resources, accumulated knowledge, traditions and our philosophy about, and perception of, the spaces in which we live.

Culture is not supposed to remain static. Traditions are not meant to stifle the accumulation and integration of new knowledge, but rather to preserve, guard and transmit the value of what it represents. For certain, culture is a weapon. It can be used as a tool to control, exploit and oppress or as a tool for liberation, exploration and freedom.

Cultures are usually developed over a period of time based on the factors cited above plus others. Cultures can also be adopted, embraced or expanded upon by those who were not the original or indigenous practitioners. We see this tendency throughout the course of human development, particularly in areas of music, food, religion, war, science and the arts. So again, culture is very important and can be utilized as a weapon. However, culture is a tool that must be used in tandem or in collaboration with other variables to be effective at developing a people or society. Embracing a set of cultural perspectives, traditions and practices will not by itself liberate the Black/New Afrikan community.

If all Black people decided to self-identify as **Afrikans** or **New Afrikans** or **Indigenous** or **Moors**: If all Black folks decided to collectively embrace and practice the **Nguzo Saba** (principles of Kwanzaa) or the **Five Pillars of Islam** or the **Ten Commandments** or the **Forty-Two Negative Confessions**: eat only **Halal** foods or go **vegan** or eat only **organically:** we would certainly be a very healthy, emotionally stable, God-conscious and spiritually balanced people..., **but we would still remain an exploited and oppressed internal colony of the United States.**

In summary, the comments above reflect the main contradiction and limitation of **Cultural Nationalism:** ignoring or marginalizing the crucial importance of political education, political activism, economic development and/or self/group defense: advocating for and promoting the idea and practice that by adapting or developing particular cultural beliefs and traditions, Blacks/New Afrikans would embody and achieve the **ultimate manifestation of victory** over white-supremacy and economic injustice.

Developing or adapting a certain set of cultural values and/or traditions will never help to free Black people unless such traditions and practices are intricately connected to our fight for freedom and self-determination. No matter how Afrikan-centered: no matter how organic: no matter how halal.

Proclaiming a specific identity alone (for example: New Afrikan, Moor, Indigenous, etc.) **will not** free us. In the United States you can basically self-identify as anything you want. Wearing Afrikan or Islamic garb does not free us either. Only by **acquiring power** and institutionalizing our power, can we truly be free. We should know and understand by now that **white-supremacy based capitalism** has a tendency to commodify and sell anything it can: from Malcolm X gear to Kwanzaa decorations to Halal grocery products to Martin Luther King Jr. holiday discount specials.

For oppressed and exploited peoples to be free, culture must be utilized as a weapon and not just as a means of entertainment, career choice and/or means to achieve fortune and fame. Cultural appropriation (such as a ceremonial Kwanzaa celebration and/or a fictional 'Wakanda' display) is no substitute for rigorous radical and revolutionary movement-building. Lighting the candles and/or crossing our arms in salute means very little if we as New Afrikans/Blacks fail to engage in building and sustaining a revolutionary culture. It must be a culture that consciously and unapologetically centers the movement and struggle for our freedom and liberation: a culture which is posed to defend the image and integrity of Black people and attack those who dare attack us.

Most importantly, at this critical juncture in our history, we need a **revolutionary culture** that is able to transcend the various ideological and philosophical tendencies within our communities. A culture that is able to acknowledge, support, incorporate and defend any individual, group, organization (for example, temple, church, mosque) as long as they are willing to fight for our collective freedom and stand in firm opposition to white-supremacy.

We need a culture that will serve as the **central ingredient or glue** for maintaining and expanding **principled and functional unity** in order to sustain our revolutionary movement.

I will be relatively brief in my comments regarding the limitations of **Pan-Afrikanism**. Much of my critique concerning the limitations of Black Nationalism is also applicable.

For example, in response to colonialism and oppression throughout Africa, we have numerous examples of successful and victorious struggles and wars for national liberation that took place throughout Africa and elsewhere following the end of World War II.

However, what we have witnessed during the post-colonial period in Africa is the development of societies that are undemocratic, oppressive and corrupt. They are headed by Africans politically, but in many ways continue to be controlled by the forces of white-supremacy economically and financially. This has been accomplished through institutions such as the International Monetary Fund, World Bank, NATO, multinational corporations, intelligence units such as the CIA and the United Nations. Collectively, they (along with corrupt African political and military leadership) continue to keep Africa fragmented, broke and dependent. Just as in the United States, the most severely impacted people are the poor and low-income.

The Black working class and poor in South Africa, for example, are now engaged in struggles with the Black post-apartheid ruling class and political parties such as the African National Congress (ANC).

The ANC was at one time recognized as the leading organization fighting against apartheid in South Africa. The ANC was the political party of Nelson Mandela and Winnie Mandela. How now has it come to represent the interest of international capitalism and the Black ruling class of South Africa?

It appears that the ideals and guiding philosophies of Pan-Afrikanism are used to promote neo-colonial hegemony throughout the African continent. Relatively new global forces such as China and the (U.S. created) AFRICOM are both solidifying and expanding their economic, cultural and military footprint in various regions of the continent as well. Just like the 1885 Berlin Conference, Africa is again up for grabs: this time with Black faces doing the auctioneering.

Much in the same way, within the **U.S. Civil Rights Movement**, certain members of its leadership went on to become staunch apologists and defenders of the United States status quo. Likewise, certain leaders and representatives of the **Black Power Movement** went on to become public officials, corporate executives and academia who emerged as beneficiaries, luke-warm critics and defenders of U.S. white supremacy, while simultaneously facilitating the development and entrenchment of a neo-colonial relationship between Black people and the U.S. ruling class. Some were unconscious collaborators while others were intentional and deliberate traitors.

Pan-Afrikanism can also cloud and obscure our analysis and practice and generate similar politically dysfunctional and counter-revolutionary scenarios. We end up cheering for and supporting totalitarian, anti-democratic and corrupt leaders because they are Africans, talk bad about white people and perhaps were revolutionaries and comrades during the anti-colonial period. Pan-Afrikanism must be guided by principles of democracy and equity, particularly regarding the distribution of wealth and opportunity. Pan-Afrikanism must take on a more pronounced and defined socialist (versus capitalist) perspective in advancing ideas of democracy and wealth distribution.

Pan-Afrikanism must reject the attempts and resist the incursions of non-Africans and corrupt Africans to re-colonize Africa. Africa has enormous developmental capacity. It also has tremendous human and mineral wealth. We must reject and resist all attempts to **re-colonize Africa** by those who will certainly exploit it in order to salvage what remains of neo-liberalism.

While we love and honor the brilliance of Marcus Garvey, Amy Ashford Garvey, Amy Jacques Garvey and the contributions and influences of the Universal Negro Improvement Association (UNIA), we must reject capitalism as a viable economic and/or social model for Black people as we embark on the remainder of the 21st century.

Pan-Afrikanism must be profoundly **socialist, anti-imperialist and internationalist** in order to remain relevant.

CHAPTER 5

Theory and Practice: Continuing the Legacy of the Black Panther Party

Introduction and Overview of the Black Panther Party

Founded in October of 1966 by Huey P. Newton and Bobby Seale as the Black Panther Party for Self-Defense, the Black Panther Party (as it came to be officially known) emerged as one of the most important and significant black militant formations of the 20th century. Inspired by the fiery and Black Nationalist teachings of Malcolm X and the various anti-colonial struggles taking place throughout the globe in the post-World War II period, Huey Newton, Bobby Seale and others embarked on the task of creating a grassroots and revolutionary organization for Blacks in the Bay area.

Borrowing from the format and style of the Nation of Islam 'What We Want: What We Believe' declarations, Huey and Bobby put together the 'Ten Point Platform and Program' of the Black Panther Party as a concise statement of strategic demands challenging not just American racism and state generated violence (the police), but the essence of U.S. political economy (capitalism, imperialism) as well.

Focusing on community patrol of the police and educating the people as to their constitutional right to bear arms, they could not have foreseen that this tiny, locally based formation would eventually and rapidly evolve into a national and international political phenomenon.

Along the way, the Black Panther Party saw its ranks grow to include people who would become legendary figures within the Black liberation movement such as Emory Douglas, Eldridge Cleaver, Elbert 'Big Man' Howard, Lil'Bobby Hutton, Bunchy Carter, John Huggins, Kathleen Cleaver, Stokely Carmichael, H.'Rap' Brown, Elmer 'Geronimo' Pratt, Fred Hampton, Mark Clark, Erica Huggins, Elaine Brown, Donald 'D.C.' Cox, George Jackson, Dhoruba Bin Wahad, Afeni Shakur, Assata Shakur, Mumia Abu Jamal, Russell 'Maroon' Shoatz, Safiyah Bukhari, Jalil Mutaqim, and so many others too numerous to identify by name. Their work, sacrifice and dedication have left an indelible impact on the history and trajectory of U.S. political discourse, Black radical activism and social development.

Continued popularity of BPP

Over the fifty years since its founding, the Black Panther Party continues to enjoy support and admiration, particularly among today's contingents of woke, conscious and activist youth. While not always agreeing with or embracing the party's ideology, many youth continue to be both motivated and inspired by the tenacity and courage of the Black Panthers. Also impressive and instructive are the various programs and projects developed and organized by the BPP to address the specific needs of the Black/New Afrikan communities of that time such as the free breakfast program for children, sickle cell testing program, community-based medical clinics, political education classes, etc.

Proliferation of recent Panther formations and their Ideological tendencies

Nowadays, there are a multitude of groups and organizations that identify themselves as the successor, inheritors, continuation and/or official representatives of the Black Panther Party. A few even call and identify themselves as **the** Black Panther Party. I won't go into a detailed name and identification of each formation, but I will identify a few ideological tendencies and/or tactical approaches. The majority of these formations are the off-spring of the **New Black Panther Party founded by Aaron Michaels of Dallas, Texas in 1989.** But in all fairness, the dominant ideological perspective and tactical approach taken by the majority of these formations was (and, unfortunately continues to be) based on the political philosophy of **Khalid Muhammad**.

Khalid Muhammad was the former national representative of the **Nation of Islam** under the leadership of Minister Farrakhan. At that time, Khalid Muhammad was a key advocate and voice for what I earlier describe as reactionary or juvenile Black Nationalism.

After departing from the Nation of Islam (NOI), he was invited to join the New Black Panther Party as his new host or home organization. Upon his acceptance and appointment to a key leadership position, many former and then current members of the Nation of Islam left and joined the New Black Panther Party (NBPP).

In his new leadership position within the NBPP, Khalid and others of similar background were able to establish an ideology and protocol that mirrored and reflected the politics and ideology of the Nation of Islam (of that time) and clearly not that of the Black Panther Party founded by Huey Newton and Bobby Seale.

To be clear, Khalid Muhammad was a great leader, speaker, organizer and advocate on behalf of Black freedom and self-determination. He was fearless in his critique and attacks against white-supremacy and state violence. May Allah (God) overlook his shortcomings and reward him for his good deeds. But, <u>ideologically</u> he was flawed and appeared to be unwilling or unable to critique himself and make adjustments in order to grow and advance the movement.

The Black Panther Party's historical practice and legacy was and continues to be essentially:

- Anti-Racist
- Anti-Capitalist
- Anti-Imperialist
- Pro-Self-Defense
- Community-Based
- Pro-Socialist

Its staunch anti-racism position was never promoted, advocated or practiced as being 'anti-white people'. The Black Panther Party was firmly **<u>pro-Palestinian</u>, <u>but never anti-Semitic or anti-Jewish.</u>** They often drew parallels between the Israeli-constructed apartheid that was imposed upon the Palestinians and the South African and southern United States style (Jim Crow) apartheid imposed upon Africans on the continent and Blacks/New Afrikans at home in the U.S.

Ideologically, the Black Panther Party transitioned from **Black Nationalism** to **Revolutionary Nationalism** to **Inter-Communalism**. This transition was heavily influenced by the pro-independence and anti-colonial movements that were taking place at the time as well as the civil rights and black power movements within the United States. At various times and conditions, the chief theoreticians for the Black Panther Party were Bobby Seale, Huey Newton, Eldridge Cleaver, George Jackson, Elaine Brown, Kathleen Cleaver and Dhoruba Bin Wahad. All of whom denounced racism, racial chauvinism and anti-Semitism, while remaining staunch defenders of the right to national liberation and self-determination for all oppressed peoples; especially Black people and other people of color (POC).

Panther formations of the current era have seized upon certain **rhetoric, imagery and practices** of the Black Panther Party throughout its organizational development and amplified them as if any one or more of these tendencies represents the totality of the Black Panther Party.

For instance, we have Panther formations who emphasize the self-defense messaging of the Black Panther Party by stressing the importance of community disaster survival, military preparedness and training. All of which is definitely important and needed during these times of white nationalist violence.

But, they must not do so to the exclusion of political education, community organizing and the establishment of survival programs that address other basic community needs such as food, clothing, shelter and education.

We have Panther formations that don't even provide any serious **weapons training and safety** component within their organizations, but do highly publicized armed community drills and marches. They have yet to realize that even basic **armed propaganda** must be organized and strategic.

Other formations emphasize a distinct cultural nationalist and bourgeois pan-Africanist politics, neither of which accurately reflects the Black Panther Party position on culture and/or the politics of the Afrikan Diaspora. Internationally, The BPP did not support colonialism or neo-colonialism. And, the BPP was most certainly not a cultural nationalist organization.

And last, but certainly not least, we have Panther formations that portray a tendency toward theoretical and rhetorical dogmatism: as if theorizing, intellectualizing (memorizing traditional Marxist-Leninist-Maoist writings) and shouting slogans is a viable replacement for strategic planning and action.

Learning from the Mistakes and Errors of the Black Panther Party

The Black Panther Party made many mistakes and errors during its tenure from 1966-1982. I will not go into pointed detail at this time, but will provide some general perspective:

1. Most notable was the strategic thinking error of underestimating the power and reach of our enemies.
2. There was the ideological error of advancing the lumpen proletariat of the Black/New Afrikan community as the 'vanguard element' within a protracted revolutionary struggle.
3. There was an error in organizational development in not aggressively recruiting more senior and knowledgeable Black activists into the ranks, especially as leadership, in order to perhaps counter some of the poor judgment and misguided decisions. The membership of the BPP, leadership included, was between 14-35 years old. At just 35 years old, Eldridge Cleaver was considered an old-head ('Papa Rage').

4. Another <u>error in organizational development</u> is that the BPP should have developed a Central Committee that was actually more representative of the Party as a national organization with central committee members from the east coast, mid-west, south east, etc. I believe that would have helped to counter and perhaps avert some of the tragedy which contributed to the BPP split and its aftermath. Such a central committee could also have served as a vehicle to checkmate some of the erratic and egotistical behavior of both Huey and Eldridge.

5. A <u>strategic and tactical error</u> was the failure of the Black Panther Party to develop an **independent political** **component** that dealt specifically with **electoral politics** and that would run candidates as members of the Black Panther Party and not the Democratic Party.

6. And finally, the <u>strategic and tactical error</u> of shutting-down all local BPP offices nationwide in order to focus human and other resources primarily on the mayoral campaign of Bobby Seale and local political races in the Oakland, California area. The Black Panther Party basically abandoned the national Black/New Afrikan community, its

BPP programs, projects, relationships, networks and the growing numbers of disillusioned and incarcerated current or former comrades. Along with the nasty and highly publicized BPP split and criminalization of former members (East Coast Panthers, BLA) and the changing international situation, this was certainly signaling the beginning of the decline in national influence and stature of the Black Panther Party

Importance of Combining Theory with Practice

In conclusion, I would like to emphasize the importance of always reinforcing our theories and ideas with practice and applicable work. The type of work that can produce an increase in social awareness, social activism and tangible, measured relief from the oppression and trauma associated with white supremacy and economic injustice. We need relief such as food, clothing, shelter, safety and security, education, health care and jobs. We need to be doing all of this work and more as we pursue the acquisition of the revolutionary power needed for obtaining national liberation. It is our duty to win or die trying. It is our duty to fight from one generation to the next until freedom is won. Long live the legacy of the Black Panther Party!

CHAPTER 6

Black Soldiers and Black Police: Serve the People or Defend the Empire

<u>**Historical participation of black soldiers**</u>: Black people have served as soldiers since the founding and creation of the United States. Blacks fought on the side of the American rebels and the continental army they eventually developed. As a matter of fact, school textbooks have taught for decades that the first adult person to be killed for striking a blow against the British was actually a Black man named Crispus Attucks.

Blacks/New Afrikans have actually served in every U.S. official or unofficial war and military conflict since the death of Crispus Attucks. That would include the following:

- American Revolutionary War
- War of 1812
- Wars of Indigenous Conquest (so-called 'Indian Wars')
- Civil War
- Mexican-American War
- Spanish-American War
- World War I

- World War II
- Korean War
- Vietnam War
- Invasion of Grenada
- Invasion of Panama
- Gulf War I
- Gulf War II
- Afghanistan

Additionally, Black/New Afrikan soldiers are currently deployed in western Africa as advisors and trainers of local military personnel against groups like Boko Haram as part of the so-called 'war on terror'. These operations are part of AFRICOM.

Issues and incidents of racial discrimination and violence:

In spite of their military service and heroic battlefield exploits and decorations, Blacks returning home from war have faced tremendous racial discrimination, and at times horrendous and targeted racist violence. For example, Black soldiers returning from World War I were literally beat, shot and in some instances hung. World war II Black vets returned from the war after defeating fascism only to find themselves confronted with the horrors of Jim Crow. The same for the Black veterans of the Korean and Vietnam Wars. Until an executive order (9981) by President Truman in response to a threatened massive demonstration (a march being organized by A. Phillip Randolph and others) on Washington, D.C., the United States military was segregated. In response to the overt racism, white-supremacy within the U.S. military and racist violence experienced upon their return, many Black vets joined the Civil Rights, Black Power and Black Liberation movements. Notable examples include Robert F. Williams, Medgar Evers and Elmer 'Geronimo' Pratt.

Fighting Americas' wars for what?

Blacks/New Afrikans have fought in U.S. wars for various reasons. In the earliest encounters, Blacks were often times offered freedom from slavery as a reward for their military service. As enslaved people, Blacks were also forced to fight with no promise of freedom in exchange. Some Blacks actually came to believe it was their patriotic duty to join the military and fight against whatever had been identified as the evil empire of the day (Fascism, Communism, and Radical Islam).

Others would join the military and fight in order to dispel racist propaganda that Blacks were cowards and not good soldiering material, somehow hoping to gain the rights and privileges of full U.S. citizenship by demonstrating their prowess in battle.

These folks saw themselves as representatives of the race and were extremely aware and conscious of their role in shaping public opinion and the perceptions of New Afrikan/Black people.

The more contemporary military is voluntary but often times motivated by white-nationalism, misguided patriotism, economic necessity, lack of opportunity, boredom, and adventure: although, there was a strong and noticeable surge in recruits during the period immediately after 911.

Since the 1950's the military has indeed emerged as one of the most racially integrated and diversified U.S. institutions with people of various races and ethnicities holding positions of rank, authority and power. Like college and professional sports (football, basketball), it remains one of the few institutions where Blacks/New Afrikans are not disproportionately represented in a negative demographic such as poverty, incarceration, income and/or wealth inequality. In other words, just like collegiate and professional football and basketball, Blacks within the United States military are generally represented in higher percentages than our population throughout the nation.

Black veterans: homeless, unemployed, incarcerated, suffering substance abuse and mental health problems: Consequently, Black vets are also disproportionately represented among military veterans experiencing homelessness, unemployment, incarceration and substance abuse and mental illness.

Historical origins of the police: Police forces within the United States originally developed as mechanisms for controlling and containing unpopular and unwanted newly arrived European immigrants in the north and the capture and containment of rebellious or runaway slaves in the south.

Jim Crow police forces: For over a hundred years or more, throughout the south and certain northern localities, white-supremacist terror groups and the local police were often indistinguishable to the Black community. Cops and sheriffs wore badges during the daylight hours and white-hoods and robes during the night. Racist police would cultivate and develop their law enforcement and political careers based on how violently they were willing to suppress the rights of Black/New Afrikan people. Notable examples such as Jim Clark, Bull Connor and Frank Rizzo stand out among this crowd.

Just like the U.S. military, police departments also were highly racially segregated. When Blacks were allowed to join a police force, they were initially prohibited from carrying guns and/or arresting white people. Oftentimes, their jurisdiction was restricted to only so-called Negro neighborhoods.

One of the demands made at some point during the Civil Rights struggle and Black Power movement was the hiring and promotion of more Black police officers. Black people thought that having more Black police would reduce the incidents of police-brutality, often committed against Black people by racist white officers. Over the last forty years or more, we have seen a significant <u>increase</u> in the number of Black rank and file officers as well as commanders and chiefs.

What we have not seen is any serious <u>decrease</u> in the number of Black people being targeted, harassed, unnecessarily arrested, beaten and/or murdered by the police. Integration or affirmative action within the law enforcement community has not benefited the Black community in a systemic or structural way.

Too many Black police support police brutality and murder by either going along with and actively participate in brutalizing people or defending pig police by looking the other way. The demographics and family dynamics within numerous Black/New Afrikan communities is such today that many of us have friends and family members who are police and law enforcement personnel. Meanwhile, police still engage the black communities, especially those that are predominantly working class and low-income in a hostile and overly aggressive manner, resembling that of an occupational army. Even Black police are subject to acts of racist police violence, at times being assaulted or even shot by fellow white cops under highly suspicious circumstances.

When being approached or confronted by the police for even the most trivial situation, Black folks are expected to conduct themselves like foreigners in another country or enemy combatants undergoing interrogation. We are not permitted to question police authority, must appear calm, even-toned and emotionally balanced no matter how ridiculous, dangerous and threatening the behavior of the police may be. We need those conscious, moral and ethical Black police officers to step up and intervene. Stop pig-police from murdering our people with no consequences. Stand up for justice. Follow those teachings and traditions that emphasize justice, fairness and reciprocity.

So, the fundamental question for Black/New Afrikan police and military personnel remains: are you going to uphold the honor, sacrifice and traditions of those that paved the way for you to have a military or enforcement career?

Those people who sought relief from white-supremacy and justice for future generations by demanding that Blacks be permitted equal opportunity and treatment within these institutions or, are you going to stand idly by and allow yourselves to be used in <u>advancing white supremacy throughout Africa</u> and terrorizing Blacks/New Afrikans here <u>within the United States</u>? Serve the People or Defend the Empire: the Choice is yours.

CHAPTER 7

Building the Movement for Freedom and Self-Determination

Below are a few closing comments in helping us to move forward in building a comprehensive movement:

The movement must be led by working class and low-income people: any genuine movement for Black freedom and self-determination must represent the interest of those within our communities who are the most vulnerable, exploited and oppressed. And, most importantly, must be led by those people as well. A movement <u>dominated</u> by celebrities, non-profit professionals and academics will not provide the radical and revolutionary leadership needed to achieve our liberation. And, to be clear, we are not anti-intellectual, but we embrace the <u>scholar-warrior</u> tradition. We support the tradition of academics and scholars who are actively engaged in pursuing radical and revolutionary change, not just staying 'published' to secure tenure or permanent employment at a college or university. While we all have a role to play, our ideological and strategic leadership must emerge from among the most dedicated and principled among us. We don't need yet another generation of neo-colonial puppets and sell-outs.

Socialist oriented: we must center socialism as the most inclusive and democratic model for Black/New Afrikan economic development.

Anti-imperialist: our movement must take a firm stand against U.S. intervention in the affairs of other countries and nations for purposes of regime change and the control of their natural resources (for example, oil, minerals). We are strongly opposed to militarism and the policy of endless war. We firmly support the rights of all oppressed peoples for national liberation and self-determination.

Identify central focus: the central focus of our movement must be the dismantling of white-supremacy.

Must both acknowledge and respect the right of self-defense: the movement must acknowledge that as an <u>oppressed group of people</u>, we have a right to engage in personal and group defense. We are being targeted for oppression because we are Black/New Afrikan people, <u>not</u> because of singular or personal characteristics <u>unconnected</u> to the identity of our group. To paraphrase and update the commentary of Malcolm X: we are not being oppressed because we are <u>EXCLUSIVELY</u> Christian, Muslim, Hebrew, Yoruba, Moor, Heterosexual, LGBTQ etc. We are being oppressed <u>PRIMARILY</u> because we are Black. Race continues to be the most dominant and salient contradiction and source of conflict within the United States. It is imperative that our movement, even as we acknowledge, recognize and repair the many self/group inflicted wounds and injustices, never lose sight of this overarching reality.

And, lastly we have got to love and respect one another... again. The impact of the 'War on Drugs' has resulted in, and amplified a ton of self-destructive thinking and behaviors among us. Distrust and disrespect now runs rampant among us. Some elements within our youth and adult population demonstrate little, if any, regard for life itself.

Love and respect is an integral component to social cohesion and unity: both are crucial to organizing and sustaining our movement for freedom and self-determination. Much love to you.

CHAPTER 8

Select Writings: 2014-2017

'Message to the Black Man': The One Living in the White-House (9/23/2014)

Listed Below is my response to a question regarding what I think President Obama could do to relieve some of the Black and poor misery throughout the United States: Your thoughts???

1. **National Campaign for Drug De-Criminalization and Amnesty. See this link for contact:** National Campaign for Drug De-Criminalization and Amnesty. End the bogus **'War on Drugs'** and effectively end **'Mass Incarceration'** as well.

2. **A comprehensive urban jobs and economic development initiative** (King-Malcolm-Chavez plan) to create jobs, spur and sustain economic development specifically in Black and Brown urban America.

3. **An immediate end to corporate-driven and imperialistic wars** in Asia, Africa and the Middle-East. Thus, freeing up billions of dollars needed for improving U.S. infrastructure, creating jobs and (small) business development.

4. **Freedom for all Political Prisoners:** especially those from the Black Panther Party, the BLA, the anti-Imperialist movements and Leonard Peltier.

5. **Universal debt relief** for all people earning less than $250,000 per year.

6. **A National Civilian-Police Review Board** which has the authority to automatically investigate (and prosecute) ALL police-involved shootings, especially those involving cities that have histories of police terror and misconduct, such as LA, NY, Philadelphia, Chicago, Dallas, Memphis, Pittsburgh and most recently, Ferguson.

7. **A comprehensive strategy to end urban fratricide**, involving conditional release and amnesty for Larry Hoover, Jeff Fort and others. Utilizing indigenous urban leadership and groups (for example, National Council for Urban Peace and Justice, Inc.) in negotiating and

solidifying a government backed and FINANCED permanent urban peace agreement. It must include resources for housing, education, training, mental health services and community based economic development (not gentrification).

If Obama, and his supporters from within the Black/New Afrikan communities, seriously think he deserves to be included within the circle of people such as King, Malcolm and Rosa Parks, he can certainly start the process for consideration by embracing and implementing the above recommendations. Otherwise, his legacy should be limited to just that of another "first".

'Politics in Command': (12/14/2014)

The New Afrikan Independence Party (NAIP) defines politics as "the struggle concerning the acquisition and distribution of power and resources". We contend that everything is political: where we live, where we work, and the schools we attend: how we vote, where and how we spend our money and how we interact with the police. The conceptualization and practice of politics is also shaped and determined by personal experiences and collective history and culture as well.

The recent developments concerning the grand-jury decisions regarding the police-state murders of **Michael Brown** and **Eric Garner** and the continued investigation into the police murder of 12 year-old **Tamir Rice** have resulted in a groundswell of protest and rebellion throughout the United States, with supportive protest and demonstrations from around the world.

We certainly support the demand for immediate justice for those families and communities directly impacted, as well as calls for *structural reform* and *police accountability*. We will continue to engage and participate in *peaceful protest* and demonstrations and respect the rights of those who engage in other forms of rebellion as well.

However, we believe that Black/New Afrikan people have a human right to engage in *self-defense* and armed-*resistance* to police-state violence. It makes no sense for Blacks to maintain faith in a criminal justice system to protect us from racist, white-supremacist and self-hating forces when many of these individuals are *embedded within* the criminal justice system itself. They serve as police, grand-jurors, district attorneys, judges and the like.

Just as we reject *unconditional non-violence and pacifism*, we also reject the *glorification of violence and war* as a substitute for political education, community-organizing and mass mobilization. We understand clearly that **revolution is a process, not an event.**

The NAIP supports the creation and proliferation of Black/New Afrikan gun clubs, rifle clubs, neighborhood patrols and community-defense groups. We understand the intended and real value of such formations, particularly those that adhere to the politics of Black liberation and self/group determination.

We understand that weapons and the use of violence are conditional tools, a means toward an end. We should always be in control via our values, beliefs, movement goals and objectives. We must not let personal disappointment and bitterness or the glorification of gun-culture define who we are. Our conditions and circumstances demand that we *organize for survival and development*. Our politics must be in command at all times.

'Collective Consciousness and Community Defense': (6/29/2015)

The murder of nine Black/New Afrikans at the historic Mother Emmanuel AME Church in Charleston, South Carolina is a heart-wrenching and incomprehensible tragedy. It should also represent a turning point in **the current struggle for Black justice and freedom in the United States.**

Political pundits throughout main-stream media outlets have struggled with articulating the reality of **racial hatred, violence and terrorism directed toward Blacks/New Afrikans**. Instead, many have focused on calling for more stringent **gun-control**

laws and the **removal of the confederate flag** from government properties, while ignoring the obvious pattern of race-based terrorism aimed at Blacks all across the United States.

Vigilantes, murderous pig-police and now, organized and armed white-supremacist have targeted and converged upon Black/New Afrikan people with a vengeance. Traditional and "responsible" African-American leadership appears to be **unprepared and ill-equipped** to respond to these most recent situations, while more radical and militant Black leaders are angry and outraged, but have so far, failed to provide **a tangible and programmatic approach.**

Calls for gun-control may be well-intended, but ultimately only help to assist in the efforts to **systematically disarm the Black/New Afrikan communities** and make it easier for Black folks to be victimized by whites and other reactionary forces within our neighborhoods.

Conversely, white folks in America are buying guns and ammunition in record numbers. Most whites are killed by other whites; however, **there are no calls for "stop the violence" or "turn in your gun"** campaigns being directed their way.

The Pittsburgh area features at least **four (4) gun-shows every year, offering discounts for children who attend with their parents.** Certain schools in the area even have gun clubs which compete against other schools. Meanwhile, predominantly Black schools (in urban areas) are only competing in traditional sports like football and basketball.

I think we all should respect and **honor the decision of surviving family members and Black clergy** in calling for understanding, non-violence and forgiveness towards the white-community in general, Dylan Roof in particular. **Forgiveness, mercy and understanding** certainly has its place and are valued characteristics of being a human being. However, so is **security, defense and group preservation.**

As we honor the memory of those who were murdered or injured and offer support to their surviving families and parishioners, we should take the time to reflect on the safety and security of Black/New Afrikan communities and institutions.

We must raise the security awareness and consciousness within our communities and neighborhoods. We must be on high-alert when it comes to those who may wish to do us harm. We must not be 'shamed' into neglecting to **educate and arm our communities and neighborhoods** regarding collective security and safety.

We cannot depend on local police, because many of these forces are **embedded with racist, violent and/or self-hating cops.** We must develop our own capacities to defend and protect ourselves. The time is now...,

All Power to The People!

Freedom in Our Lifetime!

Khalid Raheem

National Chairman

'Presidential Politics: the Lesser of two Evils is still Evil...' (11/6/2016)

As the 2016 U. S. presidential race comes to a conclusion, one thing that should be crystal clear: Blacks/New Afrikans must organize and fight for our right to **self-determination**, politically and otherwise.

The **Democratic Party** continues to manipulate and exploit the civil rights history and sentiments of the Black community, especially the baby-boomers, who are holding on to the unfulfilled promises and lofty expectations made by the democratic presidential administrations of their youth.

Just as the **Republican Party** betrayed and abandoned New Afrikans in the years **after the U.S. civil war,** so has the **Democratic Party** betrayed and manipulated New Afrikans during and since the **1960's post-civil rights era**.

Neither Hillary Clinton nor Donald Trump represents any profound change for Blacks in the United States. **Black freedom and self/group determination are not part of their agenda**.

They are both supporters and defenders of white-supremacy and economic exploitation at home (capitalism) and abroad (imperialism).

They **ONLY** differ with one another on **how best to manage the American empire,** but both agree that it needs to be defended, maintained and expanded.

All Power to The People!

Free The Land!

Free All Political Prisoners!

'Free The Land': (2/27/2015)

The call **"Free the Land"** was popularized by the **Republic of New Afrika (RNA)** in its declaration for autonomy and eventual sovereignty over the proposed five-state area **(Alabama, Mississippi, Louisiana, Georgia, and South Carolina)** that would constitute an independent Black/New Afrikan nation.

Based on the history of slavery, resistance, economic exploitation and the numerous Black-majority populated counties throughout the region, the call for an independent Black/New Afrikan state provided a much needed focus on building a **revolutionary movement** with a very specific **cultural and political identity.**

In today's post-industrialized America, the majority of Black people continue to live in the south, with some individuals and families just having returned over the last couple of decades. However, many Blacks/New Afrikans now live throughout the entire United States, with huge populations located in urban centers such as **New York, Detroit, Philadelphia, Chicago and Los Angeles.**

These populations of Blacks/New Afrikans, decades removed from the horrors of **'Jim Crow'** violence and economic exploitation, now face the challenges of chronic unemployment, community-violence, underemployment, police brutality and terror, failed public schools and mass incarceration.

Similar to the forced and involuntary migrations from the south decades ago, many Blacks/New Afrikans are being forced to migrate from their Black-majority neighborhoods because of land development policies and gentrification which favor the wealthy and elite. Suddenly, the low-income Black-majority neighborhoods have become attractive real estate for wealthy developers in collaboration with corporations and politicians in their efforts to attract mostly white, urban millennials at the expense of the working-class and poor.

In suburban and outlying areas, residents are discovering that gas-drilling companies of various sizes are offering top dollar for their lands as well. Environmental destruction, fracking and contaminated waters have become the negative by-products of such deals.

As the United States has embraced <u>mass incarceration as a strategic response</u> to controlling the poor and marginalized, more lands have been targeted for prison construction and expansion. This has occurred at the expense of building schools, child-development centers and community-health centers.

Against these multiple backdrops, the call to **"free the land"** must take on additional meaning and definition.

We must continue to fight for the fundamental freedom to control the political-economy of the historic **'black-belt south'** and __all communities__ that we, as Blacks/New Afrikans, live in.

But, we must also **'free the land'** from the ravages of urban poverty, human displacement and gentrification. We must also fight to **'free the land'** from the environmental destruction, displacement of nature and poisoning which accompanies global-warming and fracking. The land provides us with far more than just our cultural and political identity. It provides us with life, nourishment and sustainability.

Free The Land!

All Power to the People!

Khalid Raheem

'Short-Term Political Victories, Long-Term Political Enslavement': (5/23/2017)

During the last few weeks there have been many Democratic Party primary elections held featuring both prominent veterans and new-comers to electoral politics. There certainly will be more primaries held in several states over the next few months as the process advances toward the general elections of November 2017.

Some of these primaries, held in districts dominated by the Democratic Party, also have significant populations of Blacks/New Afrikans as well. As such, the general assumption is that whoever wins the democratic primary is the de-facto victor in the general election.

Within the circles of Black/New Afrikan, radical, progressive and leftist politics, no recent primary has received more attention, scrutiny and general support than that of Chokwe Antar Lumumba in his quest to become mayor of Jackson, Mississippi.

Chokwe Antar is the son of the late Chokwe Lumumba, a long-time human rights and revolutionary activist/attorney, himself a former city councilman and mayor of Jackson.

To the credit of his campaign organizers, supporters and the legacy of grassroots advocacy and organizing through formations such as the New Afrikan Peoples Organization, Malcolm X

Grassroots Movement and Cooperation Jackson, Chokwe Antar Lumumba won the Democratic mayoral primary on May 2, 2017 and appears to be on his way to becoming the next mayor of Jackson, Mississippi.

And while we commend and congratulate Brother Chokwe Antar Lumumba for his decisive primary victory, there remain some very important strategic issues concerning the quest for Black/New Afrikan freedom and self-determination.

A central issue however continues to be the need to develop a truly independent political vehicle, i.e. political party in Jackson and the surrounding cities, counties and states.

Why has this not happened? And, why is there continued dependence and reliance on the traditional Democratic Party machine and mechanism in areas that are predominantly Black/New Afrikan?

The Democratic Party is a political party of racism, capitalist exploitation, imperialism and war.

Throughout the United States, in countless cities, the dominant political party directly overseeing the deluge of Black poverty, unemployment, crime, police brutality and terror, closed schools, mass incarceration and gentrification has been the Democratic Party.

We can do better and chart a new course on developing and sustaining genuinely independent Black/New Afrikan political institutions.

Jackson, Mississippi is over eighty percent (80%) Black. We must challenge the stranglehold and hegemony of the Democratic Party over the Black/New Afrikan community. It is time to leave the political plantation of the Democratic Party and free the land.

All Power to The People!

Free The Land!

Khalid Raheem, Founder & Chairman

New Afrikan Independence Party